# BATMAN THE RETURN OF BRUCE WAYNE

Robbin Brosterman  Design Director – Books

Eddie Berganza  Executive Editor
Bob Harras  VP – Editor-in-Chief

Diane Nelson  President
Dan DiDio and Jim Lee  Co-Publishers
Geoff Johns  Chief Creative Officer
John Rood  Executive VP – Sales, Marketing and
Business Development
Amy Genkins  Senior VP – Business and Legal Affairs
Nairi Gardiner  Senior VP – Finance
Jeff Boison  VP – Publishing Operations
Mark Chiarello  VP – Art Direction and Design
John Cunningham  VP – Marketing
Terri Cunningham  VP – Talent Relations and Services
Alison Gill  Senior VP – Manufacturing and Operations
David Hyde  VP – Publicity
Hank Kanalz  Senior VP – Digital
Jay Kogan  VP – Business and Legal Affairs, Publishing
Jack Mahan  VP – Business Affairs, Talent
Nick Napolitano  VP – Manufacturing Administration
Sue Pohja  VP – Book Sales
Courtney Simmons  Senior VP – Publicity
Bob Wayne  Senior VP – Sales

Cover color by Brad Anderson.

BATMAN: THE RETURN OF BRUCE WAYNE

DC Comics
1700 Broadway, New York, NY 10019
A Warner Bros. Entertainment Company.
Printed by RR Donnelley, Salem, VA, USA 12/7/11. First Printing.
ISBN: 978-1-4012-3382-2

# THE RETURN OF BRUCE WAYNE

"GOD BE GOOD TO THE MAN IN BLACK
WHO GUARDS THE DOOR AND KEEPS THAT KEY.

"BUT SPARE ME HIS DREAD RETURN
AND WHAT MUST COME NEXT..."

HOW IS IT SO HARD TO *LOOK* AT?

DA-MAN.

≫SHUSH≪ OLD MAN SAID IT'S *HOLY.*

THINGS *HAPPEN* HERE THAT *CAN'T* HAPPEN OTHER WHERES.

THERE'S HOLY AND THERE'S *HAUNTED*...

IT'S A *SHINING-CART.*

SAME AS BROUGHT DOWN THE *FIRE*, IN OLD MAN'S STORY.

"MADE WITHOUT STITCH OR SEAM."

SO WHAT'S IT MADE OF? *SKY?*

LIKE A FLAKE OFF *SKIN* OR *FLINT?*

IT'S THE SAME BLUE *SKY* IS.

SKY'S *DIFFERENT* BLUE.

MORE LIGHTNESS IN IT.

AH, BUT SKY'S *ALL* DIFFERENT.

STAY.

*THIS* IS WHAT BLUE IT WAS WHEN IT FIRST *FELL.*

WE'RE TOO FAR FROM *DEER PEOPLE* COUNTRY.

*BLOOD MOB* BOUNDARY'S OVER *THAT RISE.*

IT'S NOT *SAFE* HERE.

EVEN THE BLOOD CHIEF *FEARS* WHAT'S HOLY.

HE'S A *DEVIL.*

HE KNOWS IF HE COMES *HERE*, IT'S *BAD LUCK* FOR HIS KIND.

BAD LUCK IF HE MEETS *ME.*

BAD LUCK FOR *US*, TOO.

HAS NOBODY SEEN *THIS* HERE?

DA?

A SKY-CART OF THE BRIGHT ONES!

FOUR SCALPS OF *DEER* WARRIORS!

AND A *MAN-GOD* WHO CAME FROM ABOVE TO CHALLENGE *ME.*

WHO WANTS TO SEE ME KILL A GOD? AND EAT HIS HEART!

FOLLOW ME!

CHIEF SAVAGE! THE DOGS, THE MEN...

...L-L-LOOK...

WHERE IS MY MAN-GOD?

SHOW YOURSELF, COWARD!

GAW!

...NO,
I CAN'T...
I...

...RRN'G'H'LYHEH...

the linear authority has vacated this station. it is no longer safe.

universal molecular motion will **cease** as **deadline time** arrives.

the local timeline terminates in **9 minutes 18 seconds.**

you **must** vacate this station.

WE TRACED **OMEGA ENERGY** HERE.

WE HOPED WE COULD USE YOUR **MAPS** OF SPACETIME TO HELP FOLLOW A **TRAIL.**

the local timeline terminates in **9 minutes 37 seconds.**

at that time our **anti-entropy aegis** will **succumb** to the unstoppable **conclusion** of the thermodynamic process.

all station information, the **complete record** of the universe-zero timeline is being packed into a **black hole** for protection.

a message in a cosmic bottle.

you arrived with moments to spare.

our maps begin with the **time point**-- without duration or span, it contains **all** possibility.

by simple **geometry,** we extend the point to create a line.

the **timeline** of **universe-zero** from beginning to end.

AND AS I'VE ALWAYS *SUSPECTED*, PERPENDICULAR TO THE *TIME PLANE* MUST BE *CUBE TIME*, FROM WHERE *WE* LOOK FLAT, EVEN *HYPERCUBE TIME*.

THINGS *LIVE* OUT THERE, I'M SURE, THINGS WITH SCALE AND DEPTH AND DIMENSIONS WE CAN ONLY BEGIN TO *IMAGINE*.

I THINK I HAD A *GLIMPSE* OF THOSE REGIONS DURING A *RECENT* ADVENTURE.

an infestation of **hyperfauna** has been detected.

the local timeline terminates in **7 minutes 14 seconds.**

LOCATE THAT *OMEGA TRAIL.*

HE'S HERE *SOMEWHERE.*

A NEEDLE IN A COSMIC HAYSTACK.

HMM

A *BAT* NAILED TO THE DOOR OF THE *CHURCH* SEEMS A SINISTER OMEN INDEED.

PERHAPS YOU'RE *RIGHT.*

I *KNOW* I AM.

*GOD HELP US ALL,* THE DEVIL WALKS AMONG US!

I *HEAR* YOU, GOODWIFE TYLER.

AND ALL OF *GOTHAM* WITH ME.

BUT STAND ASIDE AND I'LL BE ABOUT MY BUSINESS IN THE LORD'S NAME.

AND THERE I SEE A RECENTLY MENDED *JERKIN.*

BELONGING TO YOUR MISSING *HUSBAND?*

MY POOR MATTHEW.

I FEAR THE *DRAGON* IN THE WOODS HAS TAKEN *HIM* AS IT TOOK THOSE *OTHER* MEN.

JUDGING BY THE *YARN,* I'D SAY THE DEVIL'S BEEN HARD AT WORK *HERE,* TOO.

AN EXCELLENT *REPAIR.*

ALTHO' I IMAGINE MATTHEW TYLER WILL HAVE NO MORE NEED OF *THIS.*

EXCEPT AS A *SHROUD* TO WARM HIS SWIFTLY COOLING BONES.

IT SEEMS THE INNOCENT *BAT* WAS THE REAL VICTIM HERE.

BUT... BUT...

THE DEVIL.

TAKE HER AWAY!

AND AS FOR *THIS* MAN!

THIS FLEMISH *PAINTER,* VAN DERM.

IT'S MY JOB TO MAINTAIN THE *REGISTER* HERE IN GOTHAM COLONY, BROTHER *MALLEUS.*

DRAGONS OR NO DRAGONS.

WITCHES OR NO WITCHES.

AAUGHFF

THAT'S *ENOUGH!*

GET HER *OUT* OF THERE, FOR GOD'S SAKE!

SHE'S *NOT* A WITCH.

PUT HER ON TRIAL FOR KILLING HER *HUSBAND* IF YOU MUST, BUT *WITCHCRAFT?*

YE WERE SENT FROM *BOSTON* BUT TEN DAYS AGO TO HELP US ROOT OUT *WITCHES* IN THE GOTHAM COLONY, WERE YE *NOT,* BROTHER MORDECAI?

DID THEY CHOOSE THE *SOFTEST* MAN THEY COULD FIND?

I SAVE MY FIRE FOR FOES WHO'VE *EARNED* IT, *BROTHER MALLEUS.*

NOT *WIDOW-WOMEN* WHO WERE MOST LIKELY *BEATEN* BY THEIR GOOD CHRISTIAN *HUSBANDS* UNTIL THEY COULD BEAR NO MORE.

*GOOD DAY TO YOU.*

LET THEM THINK AS THEY LIKE.

IF THEY *FEAR* ME, THEY'LL LEAVE ME *ALONE.*

*NATURE* HAS BEEN A BETTER FRIEND TO ME THAN MAN.

GOD HIMSELF *REJECTED* ME WHEN I LOST MY PARENTS DURING THE SEA CROSSING FROM *BRISTOL.*

THEY CALLED US *STRANGERS,* NOT *SAINTS,* LIKE *THEMSELVES,* THE GOOD BAPTISTS.

AND NONE OF THEM WILL *ENGAGE* WITH ME SINCE THAT DAY.

THUS I LIVE, *SHUNNED.*

UNTIL *YOU* CAME.

AND MOST TIMES, I FAIL TO UNDERSTAND WHY ALL OF THIS HAS HAPPENED TO *ME.*

THEN WE HAVE SOMETHING *ELSE* IN COMMON, ANNIE...

BOTH OF US *LOST* IN OUR WAY.

MAKE SURE THE **BOOK** IS DRAWN IN YOUR SKETCH, BROTHER MARTIN.

I NEED TO **REMEMBER** IT AND WHAT I'VE **WRITTEN.**

THIS WILL BE THE BASIS FOR A WORTHY STUDY IN **OILS**, BROTHER MORDECAI, SUCH AS I LEARNED TO MAKE AT THE TABLE OF **VAN RIJN** IN ROTTERDAM.

I SEE YOU'VE TAKEN MANY **SCARS** IN THE DEFENSE OF GOD'S CREATURES.

HOW CAME YOU TO **HIS** SERVICE?

I...I'M NOT CERTAIN...

I WAS **WAYLAID** ON THE ROAD TO GOTHAM AND I REMEMBER VERY **LITTLE** PRIOR TO MY ARRIVAL.

LUCKILY, MY COMING WAS **EXPECTED...**

**HERE** HE IS.

OUR BROTHER **MORDECAI,** TOILING IN GOD'S GREAT SERVICE.

I DON'T BELIEVE THERE *ARE* WITCHES HERE.

HAVE A *CARE*, BROTHER MORDECAI.

THE DEVIL NEVER *SLEEPS*.

YOU'RE AWARE AS *I* AM THAT A WITCH IS KNOWN BY CERTAIN *SIGNS* SUCH AS THE PRESENCE OF A *FAMILIAR* OR BY SOME *BODILY* MALFORMATION...

ALL AGREE THY SPEECH IS *STRANGER* EVEN THAN THE DUTCHMAN'S HERE.

AS IF THE *KING'S ENGLISH* WERE NOT THY *NATIVE* TONGUE.

AYE, *YOU!* IS THE LORD'S GOOD CREATION NOT *SUFFICIENT,* YE MUST MAKE A CORRUPTION AND A MOCK OF IT IN CHARCOALS AND OIL?

*TCHAA!*

ATTEND TO THY VANITY IF IT SO PLEASES YE, BROTHER MORDECAI.

THE *DRAGON* HAS BEEN SIGHTED IN THE FOREST WEST OF *BRISTOL BAY.*

I HAVE WHAT I NEED TO CONTINUE.

I MUST GO *WITH* THEM, BROTHER MARTIN.

IF THERE *IS* A DRAGON, I OWE IT AN *APOLOGY.*

KEEP MY BOOK SAFE.

...THE *HIDDEN PEOPLE* WHO WERE HERE BEFORE US CALL THEMSELVES *MIAGANI.*

IT MEANS *BAT-PEOPLE.*

BAT-PEOPLE?

ALWAYS *BATS,* OF COURSE.

I *KNOW* THESE CAVES.

ANNIE, I'M NOT *FROM* HERE, I'M NOT *MORDECAI.*

I'M SOMEBODY *ELSE*...FROM FAR AWAY...AND YET I *KNOW* THESE CAVES...

IT WAS *YOU,* WASN'T IT?

YOU WEREN'T GATHERING *HERBS* IN THE GROVE WHEN YOU FOUND ME.

*YOU* SUMMONED THE DRAGON AND IT KILLED THE *REAL* MORDECAI.

THEY SENT HIM TO *HUNT* ME!

I ONLY WANTED TO CHASE THEM ALL *AWAY.*

ALL THOSE PIOUS *SAINTS* WHO CUT DOWN *SACRED TREES* AND SLAUGHTER THE *BROTHER ANIMALS* AND STEAL FROM THE BAT-PEOPLE WHOSE LAND THIS *IS.*

...IN THE WATER.

ANNIE, RUN! THIS IS NO GOD OR DEVIL!

RUN!

RUN!

WHATEVER IT IS, I BROUGHT IT HERE! IT'S MY RESPONSIBILITY.

ARE THESE *CHRISTIAN* SIGNS?

OR SEALS OF THE *DEVIL'S* APOSTATE THRONG?

*GOODWIFE TYLER* SPOKE IN EARNEST.

THE SOURCE OF GOTHAM TOWN'S ILLS REVEALED!

AND I'LL VOW *BROTHER MORDECAI* WAS TEMPTED BY THIS *JEZEBEL* TO HIS *DEATH* AT THE DRAGON'S CLAWS.

THERE'S BUT *ONE* WAY TO END THIS. FIRE.

YOU DON'T UNDERSTAND!

YOU HAVE TO HELP HIM!

SOMEBODY HELP HIM!

GNHUUH

URRH!

YOU DON'T LIKE *THAT*, DO YOU?

*GGRRRAAA*

≥HFF≥
≥HFF≥

ANNIE!

SOMETHING TERRIBLE IS HAPPENING.

That Fall, the harvest was good.

Word went around that Brother Mordecai had perished while slaying the dragon of Colony Hill.

Word soon became legend.

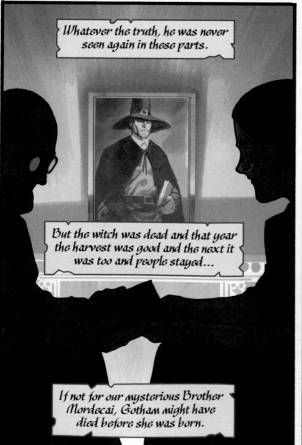

Whatever the truth, he was never seen again in these parts.

But the witch was dead and that year the harvest was good and the next it was too and people stayed...

If not for our mysterious Brother Mordecai, Gotham might have died before she was born.

As for the Devil, that was another matter altogether...

The Devil was not yet done with Gotham.

REMEMBER.

*Being the journal of Jack Valor, year of Our Lord 1734.*

IS HE MAKING ANY *SENSE* YET?

HERE!

LET'S I *SEE* HIM!

THE *BLACK PIRATE*, AS I LIVE AND BREATHE!

DIDN'T I *TELL* YOU HE WAS NO GHOST?

STICK WITH *BLACKBEARD*, BOYS.

YOU WON'T GO WRONG.

*The unhappy circumstances in which I found myself that dreadful stormy night are etched forever into my memory, along with the faces and the voices of Blackbeard... and that other man...*

CAT TORE OUT YER *TONGUE?*

STRUCK *MUTE,* ARE YOU, BY THE SIGHT OF BOLD *BLACKBEARD'S* MEN?

HEH.

DON'T *FORGET.*

...that ghost who seems to haunt me still.

WHAT'S *THIS?*

A SHIP OF *PATCHES...* A SUIT OF *RAGS...*

WHO PUT *THESE* ON YOUR BACK?

YOU LOOK LIKE--

*UNNGH!*

STRONG, TOO.

BUT RAISE THEM HANDS TO ME *AGAIN*, I'LL HAVE THEM *CHOPPED* AT THE WRISTS.

NOW *DO YOU* *DENY* YOU ARE THE *BLACK PIRATE*?

*RRRR*

I'VE HAD *FLEAS* BITE WORSE.

BUT I'LL TAKE THAT TO MEAN YOU *ARE*, THEN.

FOR THAT'S *YOUR* SHIP, THE *BLACK ROSE*, ALL SMASHED UP ON *BRISTOL ROCKS*.

AND THERE'S *MINE*, THE *REVENGE*, SAFE ON THE EDGE OF THE STORM.

NOW I DIDN'T COME *ALL THAT WAY* AND WASTE ALL THAT *SHOT* ON YE FOR NAUGHT, DID I?

THEY SAID YOU WAS A *GHOST*, AND I THINK I'VE SET 'EM RIGHT ON *THAT* SCORE.

BLACK PIRATE, SPIRIT OF THE SEAS--*HAH!*

AND NOW IF THE BLACK PIRATE'S *REAL*...

THEN SO'S THAT FABLED INDIAN *TREASURE HOARD* THEY SAY HE KEEPS TO *HIMSELF*.

SOMEWHERE HIDDEN IN THE *GOTHAM COUNTY CATACOMBS*, THEY SAY.

NOBODY WHO WENT IN *SEARCH* OF IT EVER *CAME BACK* TO TELL THE TALE.

ONLY A *GHOST* KNOWS THE WAY.

AND *HERE* HE IS, NURSING HIS *BRUISES*.

IF I KNEW WHERE *TREASURE* WAS I'D SHOW YOU.

YOU HAVE THE *WRONG MAN*.

YOU WOULDN'T CUT THE THROAT OF YOUR *GREATEST ADMIRER!*

HTT!

GIVE HIM A *CHANCE,* HE CALLS ME "COMMODORE."

RESPECT.

THAT'LL TAKE YOU A LONG WAY.

SO YOU *KNOW* OF ME, BOY?

WHO HASN'T HEARD OF COMMODORE THATCH?

ON *NEW PROVIDENCE* YOUR NAME IS LEGEND.

'TWAS YOUR *INSPIRATION* THAT BROUGHT ME TO *SEA* WITH THE PIRATES!

LET HIM GO.

I'LL *FIND* YOUR TREASURE.

NOBODY HAS TO GET HURT.

I'LL TAKE YOU INTO THE CATACOMBS.

LET THE BOY GO.

SIR, I AM *FIFTEEN YEARS OLD!*

AND MY NAME IS *JACK LOGGINS!*

GO, SAYS YOU?

THEN SAYS I LET HIM *JOIN* US ON OUR JOURNEY TO THE UNDERWORLD.

AND I PLACE YOUNG *MASTER LOGGINS'S* LIFE IN YOUR CAPABLE HANDS, "BLACK PIRATE."

LEAD ON.

*If my actions seem at all heroic, consider this--I knew Thatch rarely, if ever, resorted to cutting the throats of his enemies.*

HERE'S A BOWL OF BEST *SMOKE* FOR THIS FINE, GRINNING DANDY.

WISH US GOOD LUCK AND A SAFE RETURN!

WITH ALL THE *LOOT* WE CAN CARRY...

WHEN THE *PILGRIMS* CAME, THE LAST OF THE DIVIDED *DEER TRIBE* RETREATED TO THE CAVES TO JOIN THE *BAT-PEOPLE.*

GHOST-PEOPLE.

SO SAYS THE LOCAL *LORE* AT LEAST.

WELL SPOKEN AND KNOWS *HISTORY!*

WHAT WOULD HIS *FAMILY* PAY IN RETURN FOR THE SAFETY OF A LAD LIKE THAT?

LOOK CLOSELY AND YOU'LL SEE THAT HIS CLOTHES ARE *SOILED* AND NOT *NEW.*

HIS HEELS ARE *WORN,* HIS BUCKLES ARE *SCUFFED* AND HIS HANDS ARE TOO *CALLOUSED* TO BELONG TO A RICH MAN.

JACK IS OF A FAMILY FALLEN ON *HARD TIMES.*

*He was a shrewd fellow and that was good luck.*

PFFF!

THEN, IT'S *TREASURE* OR NOTHING AT ALL.

*But how could he know about the terrible traps the Miagani had set?*

AS...AS THE *BLACK PIRATE* YOU'LL KNOW *ALL* THE NAMES OF ALL THE MIAGANI TRAPS AND SNARES FROM THE OLD TALES.

I THINK I WANT *THIS* WAY.

STOP. WHAT *NAMES*, JACK?

THE *WHISTLING DEMON.* THE *BREATH OF THE BAT.*

THE *BRIDGE OF BONES.* OR SO I HEARD.

THE *RIVER OF...OF NIGHT.*

WHY'S HE *STOP* SO MUCH IF HE *KNOWS* THE WAY?

HH

ECHOES.

DEAD MEN AHEAD.

AND THE TORCH IS *FLARING...*

WHO RESETS THE SNARES IF NOT *YOU?*

PERHAPS THERE IS A *REAL* GHOST, SIR!

THEY SAY *JON VALOR, THE BLACK PIRATE* DIED NEAR A HUNDRED YEARS AGO!

*I'M* TALKING, BOY!

NEVER YOU MIND BREATH OF BAT AND CLAW OF RAT AND ALL THAT JABBER.

WHY'S *HE* HAVING TO THINK SO HARD ABOUT THE WAY?

THOSE ARE BAT-DROPPINGS.

THE METHANE WILL *ASPHYXIATE* US...

*THAT'S* WHAT KILLED THESE MEN, NOT GHOSTS.

AND...AND CERTAIN STONES ARE NOT *LEVEL.*

METHANE IS HIGHLY FLAMMABLE SO PUT OUT YOUR TORCHES, TAKE AS DEEP A BREATH AS YOU'RE ABLE TO AND MOVE VERY, VERY *CAREFULLY.*

IF YOU VALUE YOUR LIVES, DO *EXACTLY* AS I DO.

AND DON'T STEP ON ANY *RAISED* STONES.

TRY TO WATCH OUT FOR THE *TOXIC FLUID-FILLED CRATERS*, ROBIN.

*BATMAN* TO *JUSTICE LEAGUE.*

WE'RE AT THE *CRIME SCENE.*

OKAY, *COMMAND-D* WAS WHERE BATMAN'S BODY WAS DISCOVERED.

WE NOW KNOW THAT BODY WAS A DUPLICATE, A *DECOY.*

WE'VE BEEN *ALL OVER* THE SITE, BUT THAT WAS BEFORE THE PUNCTURES ON THE *RELIC* SENT ME BACK TO CHECK SOME-THING.

WITH NO NEWS FROM *SUPERMAN* AND THE OTHERS SINCE THEY LEFT *EN ROUTE* FOR THE *END OF TIME,* WE'RE OFFICIALLY ON *BLACK ALERT.*

NATURALLY WE DON'T WANT TO *ALARM* ANYONE, BUT WE ALL KNOW HOW *RESOURCEFUL* BATMAN CAN BE.

IF HE *WANTS* TO RETURN, WE HAVE TO ASSUME HE'LL BE HARD TO *STOP.*

OUR JOB IS TO DO *JUST THAT.*

NOW, IF WE REALLY HAVE TO FACE A WORLD-THREATENING ROGUE *BATMAN,* WHO BETTER THAN A FORMER *PARTNER* TO HELP PREPARE OUR STRATEGY?

*RED ROBIN,* OVER TO YOU.

THANKS, *WONDER WOMAN,* I'LL DO WHAT I CAN.

I GUESS I ALWAYS *KNEW* HE COULD GET OUT OF *ANYTHING,* EVEN THIS.

I FOLLOWED HIS *TRACES,* THE NEW BATMAN... AND ROBIN DID, TOO, JUST LIKE HE *TAUGHT* US.

WE FOUND *BAT-SYMBOLS* CARRIED BACK ACROSS THE SIBERIAN LAND BRIDGE INTO EUROPE BY NORTH AMERICAN *CAVEMEN* AND BUILT INTO 19TH CENTURY *GARDENS...*

...ALL THE CLUES LED US TO THE *RELIC...*

*NOMEX* FIRE RESISTANT FABRIC, *KEVLAR* HOOD WITH BUILT-IN ELECTRONICS.

IT SURVIVED *40 THOUSAND YEARS* IN A CAVE SO IT'S INCREDIBLY *FRAGILE...*

...BUT WE THINK WE FOUND A WAY TO BRING IT OUT FOR *CLOSE ANALYSIS.*

THE HOLES IN BATMAN'S *HELMET* MATCH THE PATTERN OF *SPIKES* IN THE CROWN.

HE GOT *OUT.*

HE GOT OUT OF THIS THING.

DON'T WE NEED TO GET BACK TO THE *JOKER?*

..."BORN FROM A BROKEN JAR", THAT'S WHAT THE CLONE BATMAN WE FOUGHT SAID...

HE GOT OUT, HE *SHOT* AND HE *WOUNDED* A GOD.

CUE THE *OMEGA EFFECT,* JUST LIKE SUPERMAN SUSPECTED, *BAM!*

HISTORY.

AUCHH

BLACK BLOODY GOD *BELOW!*

CLEAN *AIR,* AT *LAST!*

SIR. I *KNOW.*

I KNOW YOU'RE *NOT* THE BLACK PIRATE AND WE HAVE BUT A LITTLE *TIME...*

THE YEAR IS *1718.*

BUT *YESTERDAY* IT WAS *1640...* SOMETHING...AND *BEFORE...* I CAN BARELY REMEMBER THE *FEVER.*

I THINK I'M RACING THROUGH *TIME* TO SOME UNKNOWN *END.*

LIKE THE *FLYING DUTCHMAN* CURSED NEVER TO *STAY* IN ONE PLACE.

AND NO, I WASN'T *ON* THAT SHIP, BUT *YOU* WERE.

SIR, *I* WAS CAPTAIN OF THE *BLACK ROSE.*

MY NAME IS NOT LOGGINS, IT IS *VALOR.*

JACK VALOR.

MY *GRANDFATHER* WAS THE FIRST BLACK PIRATE, AND I *FOLLOWED* HIS LEAD.

LIGHT ME UP!

THIS'LL PUT FRIGHT TO *ANY* GHOST OR *INJUN!*

HRFF... WHAT'S THEY TWO *AT?!*

HHHHHH

IT'S ONLY HIM!

WHAT'S WRONG WITH YOU?

HE'S NO MORE GHOST THAN THESE BONES IS OURS!

BE YE GHOST OR MAN, I'LL HAVE MY DUE!

FOR I NEVER MET A GHOST I COULDN'T KILL!

HAR!

GNUGT

STOP OR THE BOY DIES, BLACK PIRATE!

I WOULDN'T TRY *THAT* IF I WERE YOU.

HANDS?

BEWARE.

I DID *WARN* YOU.

I ADVISE YOU TO MOVE NOT A *SINGLE FIBER* OF YOUR BEING, MISTER HANDS.

NUHH!

WHAT DAMNED KIND OF MOVE WAS *THAT*?

IT IS BY VIRTUE *ALONE* OF MY GREAT RESPECT FOR YOUR *COURAGE* THAT YOU STILL LIVE, COMMODORE.

WERE I TO UTTER A *SINGLE* WHISTLE IN THE LANGUAGE OF THE *MIAGANI*, YOU WOULD LIE *DEAD* WITH A *POISON ARROW* IN YOUR EYESOCKET.

YOU? THE *BLACK PIRATE*.

HAHAHAH

MISTER HANDS.

YOU FIRST.

TIME TO FACE THE *RIVER OF NIGHT*.

*NAHHH!* NOT THE RIVER OF NIGHT!

SO WHERE'S THE *TREASURE?!*

WE'LL *SPLIT* IT, BOY!

THERE'S NOTHING FOR *YOU* HERE BUT *DEATH*, IF YOU REMAIN A SINGLE INSTANT PAST THE VERY NEXT.

IT SEEMS YOUR DESTINY WAS TO *DELIVER* TREASURE NOT *PLUNDER* IT.

THINK YOURSELF *PRIVILEGED* TO HAVE COME THIS FAR AND YET BE ALLOWED TO *DEPART*, COMMODORE.

*GRAAA!*

THEY'RE THE LAST OF THE *MIAGANI*.

THEY CLAIM DIRECT DESCENT FROM THE *FIRST BOY*.

THEY'VE PERMITTED ME TO *HIDE* IN OTHER PARTS OF THEIR CAVES FOR MANY YEARS.

SUPERSONIC WHISTLES TO HERD THE BATS.

INCREDIBLE.

THAT CARVING IS THEIR *GOD*. PART MAN, PART BAT, *"LORD OF THE NIGHT AND THE DARK SUN."*

THEY WON'T ALLOW *ME* TO FOLLOW BEYOND THIS POINT.

BUT THEY SAY THEY RECOGNIZED *YOU*.

THEY WANT YOU TO SEE SOME SORT OF *GREAT MYSTERY* SO YOU'LL KNOW THEY'VE DONE THEIR *DUTY*.

AS LONG AS IT *NEVER LEAVES* THIS PLACE, THEY SAY IT HOLDS BACK THE *TERRIBLE DAY...*

THE *"ALL-OVER."*

ME.
I WORE THIS.
ME.

AND MIAGANI, ANNIE, MAN OF BATS

MAN

OF BATS...

FAHH! WE BEEN *LUCKY*, ISRAEL HANDS, YOU AND I, AND MAY IT LONG *CONTINUE*!

*LIFE* IS TREASURE ENOUGH FOR MEN LIKE US, THAT'S WHAT I TELL MYSELF.

I'D JUST AS SOON BE BACK ABOARD THE *REVENGE* AND FAR FROM *THIS* HAUNTED COVE, MASTER THATCH.

THAT'S ALL I'M SAYING.

ELEVEN GOOD MEN DOWN!

THIS GOTHAM'S A *BAD PLACE.*

SOME PLACES ARE BORN UNDER A BLACK SUN.

BRING ON TOMORROW WE'LL *SEIZ* IT BY THE THROAT!

...I HOPED I'D *RETIRE* OFF THAT BLACK PIRATE'S FORTUNE, MARRY MARY AND RAISE LITTLE DEVILS ON A *DESERT ISLAND* WITH BEACHES OF GOLD AND SILVER.

NEVER TRUST YOUR LIFE TO AN OLD MAN'S FOOLISH *DREAMS*, ISRAEL.

IT'S BACK TO THE *PLUNDERIN'* LIFE FOR YOU AND I!

*Some say that when they put Thatch to the gallows two months later, the golden age of piracy was over, but I say there can be no golden age to murder and greed.*

With the ghost's last instruction ringing in my ears, I spent many more years in my role as the Black Pirate, saving many a life that would not otherwise have been saved, so all that is good.

And then I met a girl.

We came to live in Philadelphia, where I left my Pirate days behind.

I never forgot the words of the ghost, and the names and the places he had me repeat and write down.

Although I must confess, I waited many years before I finally made my extraordinary journey on his behalf.

The Van Derms were a wealthy brother and sister in Gotham Town across Bristol Bay where my adventure with Thatch had taken place all those years ago.

They knew of the Miagani and instructed me to consign my papers solemnly within a casket marked with a bat-design, stepping back as if afraid when I did so.

I caught sight of an old book and...something more, of which I cannot speak.

And here it might seem the last curious ripples of that long ago day with Thatch and the ghost were finally faded, expired upon the shore...

Except for that final thing...

For all the way home, I felt a shadow at my heels, as though I had taken part in some midnight, awful rite.

And all the way home I seemed to hear bells tolling, far off in the night.

If I listen closely, I can still hear them now.

The bells of the All-Over.

JEEZ IN LOUISIANA! DID YOU *HEAR* THAT!

WHY THE HELL DID HE HAVE TO MEET US *HERE?*

PLACE BEEN HAUNTED SINCE JUDGE SOLOMON'S *BROTHER* DIED IN THE CAVES.

ENOUGH!

TAKE A LOOKIE *HERE.*

LOOK AT THAT OLD *HAUNTED HOUSE.*

NEVER FINISHED, LEFT TO ROT.

BIG-TIME SPOOKY *GUNSLINGER* JUST LIKES TO MAKE AN *IMPRESSION,* THAT'S ALL.

I DON'T LIKE THE WAY MY WHOLE LIFE'S BEEN *GOING* SINCE WE WAS OUT *WEST.*

I DON'T *LIKE* THIS.

COME INTO MY PARLOR.

BEEN LAYING OUT A *HAND* FOR YOU BOYS.

CUT THE CRAP, HEX. IS THAT REALLY *YOU?*

...KINDA HARD TO MISTAKE ME FOR SOMEBODY *ELSE.*

I FIGURED YA'LL'D BE MEN OF *REASON,* NOT *SUPERSTITION,* IF YA HAD THE GUTS TO MEET ON CURSED AND *HAUNTED* GROUND.

SO YOU'RE *NOT,* ARE YA?

SUPERSTITIOUS.

THEY SAY JONAH HEX IS THE BEST BOUNTY HUNTER AROUND. THEY SAY YOU BRING *BAD LUCK* ON YOUR TARGETS.

OUR BOSS HAS MONEY, GOLD, RIGHT *HERE...*

TELL HIM ABOUT THE *STRANGER...*

WILL YOU SHUT *UP!*

HEX, WE BROUGHT SOME KINDA FURY DOWN ON OUR HEADS, NEVER *TIRES,* NEVER *STOPS.*

I DUG *THIS* OUT OF MY IMBECILE BROTHER HERE'S *SHOULDER-BLADE.*

COULDN'T SHOOT A GUN FOR *THREE* DAYS.

OUR *BOSS* HAS PROMISED TO PAY *TRIPLE* WHAT'S IN THE BAG IF YOU PUT THIS SINISTER *HOMBRE* IN A DEEP HOLE WHERE HE BELONGS.

THEY SAY YOU'RE THE *GREATEST,* HEX...

...THEY SAY AIN'T NOBODY FASTER.

YOU READY TO *PROVE* THAT?

BATMAN: BRUCE WAYNE

PART FOUR
DARK NIGHT,
DARK RIDER

LAUDANUM.

FOR THE *PAIN,* YOU UNDERSTAND.

I *CAN'T DIE* AND NEITHER CAN THE *CANCER* IN MY GUT.

BONSOIR, MR. HEX.

CUT YOURSELF *SHAVING?*

I'D *OFFER* TO SHARE, BUT I'D HATE TO SPOIL YOUR FAMOUS *AIM.*

I'LL PASS.

YA HIRED ME TO KILL SOME *MYSTERY MAN* WON'T LEAVE Y'ALL *ALONE,* AM I RIGHT? YOU RECKON HE AIN'T GONNA *STOP* 'LESS I PUT HIM DOWN.

I CAN'T GET NUTHIN' STRAIGHT OUTTA *THEM TWO.*

CHUCK AND LUCKY ONLY KNOW WHAT THEIR VESTIGIAL BRAINS CAN *HANDLE.*

A *COWBOY IN BLACK* FOLLOWED THIS BRACE OF DISMAL TROLLS LIKE A STINK THEY COULDN'T SHAKE, AND NOW HE'S YOUR *PROBLEM.*

WE'RE *BUSY* MEN HERE.

YOU'RE *PAYING.*

WHUT'S BEHIND THE *DOOR?*

SOMEBODY BURNING *SAGE SNNFF* AND SUMTHIN *ELSE* I CAN'T TELL...

IT'S COMPLICATED, HEX.

..IF YOU ONLY KNEW...HOW THAT DWARF BONAPARTE BETRAYED ME...

THEY ALL BETRAY ME IN--AH!

...SHE'LL TALK SOON ENOUGH.

YOU DON'T NEED ME ANYMORE.

YOU DIDN'T SAY NOTHING ABOUT BAT-PEOPLE.

THESE PEOPLE HAVE SECRETS TO TURN THE SKY UPSIDE DOWN.

YOU OPEN THAT BOX, IT'S THE END OF THE WORLD.

END OF THE WORLD'S EXTRA.

TAKE WHAT YOU NEED TO SOFTEN THE BLOW, HEX.

AND THERE'S MORE.

THERE'S ALWAYS MORE.

JUST AS SOON AS YOU LAY OUR DEMON TO REST.

I CAN'T SEE WHAT'S **GOING** ON!

SO GET **OUT** THERE AND **FIND** OUT!

LUCKY!

HE WAS **THERE**! I **SAW** HIM!

KRAK

I KNOW I **SAW** HIM RIGHT...

...THERE...

YOU HEAR THAT? THIS IS NO **ORDINARY** MAN. HE'S COME FOR THE **BOX!**

WHUT'S **HE** BEEN CHEWIN'?

**MONEY** OR **ANSWERS**, HEX, YOU TAKES YOUR **CHOICE**. THE RED MAN'S TALKING ABOUT AN **OLDER** WORLD THAN YOU CAN EVER KNOW.

WHY WON'T HE LEAVE US **BE?**

BUCKY **NEVER** SHOULD HAVE **SHOT** THAT KID! I CAN **STILL** SEE HIM.

**FACE** YOUR FEARS, BOYS. HE DOESN'T CARE ABOUT **YOU.**

IT'S WHAT'S IN THAT **BOX.**

AT LEAST... GIVE US HEX.

HE'S HERE FOR **MY** PROTECTION NOT **YOURS**, YOU CHICKEN-LIVERED SPAWN OF GOMORRAH!

**GET** OUT THERE AND BRING ME THE MYSTERY MAN SO HEX CAN SHOOT HIM DEAD!

AS FOR **YOU**, GET BACK WHERE YOU'RE NEEDED!

**OPEN** THAT BOX AND BE DONE! THE END OF THE WORLD COULD ONLY COME AS A **RELIEF!**

HUH? CHUCK. *WHERE ARE YOU?*

UKT.

I THINK I *HEAR* HIM.

HELP ME OUT HERE!

STAY BACK, COWBOY! *I'LL SHOOT AND I'LL KEEP SHOOTING!*

BUT IT'S...

OH, MY DEAR LORD.

MY MOMMA WOULDN'T *EVER* HAVE PARTED WITH *THIS.*

NOT 'LESS SHE *SENT* YOU.

THIS IS FROM THE *OLDEN DAYS.*

THAT MEANS IT'S *NOW.*

OH GOD. "ALL THE DAYS OF THE WORLD IS ONE DAY AND HE MUST BE STRONG FOR US ALL!"

GRAN'PA JEROME *WASN'T* MAD...

SEE?

♪♪

*HE* TAUGHT ME.

IT'S THE *END*, SURE...BUT AS LONG AS THE *STRANGER* GETS THE *BOX*...

...EVERYTHING WILL SURELY WORK OUT, RIGHT?

In the transitory silence that followed that sickening, awful impact one thing was certain: what had but a moment earlier assumed the character of a wraith, a vengeful demon of timeless judgment...

...was flesh...

...was blood.

I reflect more often than is comfortable for my disposition upon how it might have been had I not ventured out that gloomy night to foolishly compose an end which was never mine to undertake.

For there was nothing of chance that night and all of a subtle, terrifying design.

A blueprint sketched in lines of circumstance that converged there, somehow, in the unfinished house of Wayne and Van Derm.

What could I do but surrender to its gravity?

NOW WHAT'D I DO?

And so we were wed.

And so was Kenneth born, our dark son, delivered from a gaping tomb.

His first breath, her last.

Perhaps we were all accursed on that bridge.

They say the bounty hunter Hex rode out west to meet his destiny, with "Bonaparte's gold" as apt payment for his part in the night's performance.

Perhaps he was the lucky one.

Of Thomas, the tales were altogether lurid and best left unrecorded.

Thomas, rumored to be 150 years old, had in every aspect appeared no more than ten years my senior.

S.S. Orion

Gotham to Liverpool

They say he too sought in blood the secret of life eternal...

...but that was blood of a different sort.

Catherine and I found eternity in the completion of the Manor house: that great design fulfilled in stone and timber.

But there remained, in the end, the question of the casket.

Concerning this item, Catherine had one final request. "Keep it safe and mark it with a bat. He must return."

It is thus in her sweet memory, I have commissioned a garden in form so grand and so macabre its wings outspread will cast a shadow across time and the dead.

For was it only me who saw in the opening of that box the sickening likeness of a coffin's lid?

Was it only me who saw a yawning vacant grave within, and something beyond, that seemed to be all our graves?

God be good to the man in black who guards the door and keeps that key.

...UHHH...

But spare me his dread return and what must come next...

I WAS *BATMAN'S* PARTNER LONGER THAN *ANYONE* ELSE.

TRUST ME-- BEING MAROONED IN THE PAST WITH NO MEMORY IS JUST ONE MORE PROBLEM FOR HIM TO SOLVE.

*DARKSEID* KNEW THAT.

HIS FINAL ACT WAS TO TURN BATMAN INTO A *WEAPON.*

BEFORE WE LOST CONTACT WITH HIS TEAM, *SUPERMAN* RETRIEVED THIS *ROCKET* FROM THE LATE *PALEOLITHIC ERA,* WITH BATMAN'S *FINGERPRINTS* ALL OVER IT.

AND A *RECORDING* THAT TOLD US EVERYTHING WE NEEDED TO KNOW.

I...I CAN'T REMEMBER MY NAME ANYMORE.

HOW THE HELL DO I GET OUT OF THIS ONE?

HE'LL *FIGHT* HIS WAY BACK LIKE HE *ALWAYS* DOES.

ACCUMULATING ENOUGH *OMEGA ENERGY* TO BLOW A *HOLE IN TIME.*

WONDER WOMAN?

YOU'VE HEARD WHAT *RED ROBIN* HAS TO SAY...

...BATMAN IS OUR *FRIEND,* BUT WE CAN'T ALLOW HIM TO ENDANGER THE SAFETY OF THE ENTIRE *WORLD.*

YOU ALL KNOW WHAT TO DO.

*When you think about it, life is like a detective story...*

*...it's all shadows and clues, mysteries and secrets.*

WHAT THE HELL *IS* THAT?

HOW DID I WIND UP IN A *HOSPITAL?*

SOMEBODY LIKE TO TELL ME WHAT'S GOING *ON?*

ONE OF THE DOCTORS CALLED *MS. LAMARR* WHEN THEY BROUGHT YOU IN.

YOU WERE *SHOT* THEN KNOCKED DOWN IN THE *STREET.*

YOU'RE LUCKY A HAIRLINE FRACTURE'S *ALL* YOU WOUND UP WITH.

YOU WILL WANT *THIS* AS A MEMENTO.

IT'S ALL LIKE OLD NOTES AND OBSERVATIONS AND STUFF.

MIGHT NOT BE *WORTH* MUCH NOW...

...BUT IT TOOK THE *BULLET* IMPACT AND SAVED YOUR *LIFE.*

HH.

GET *READY* AND MEET ME *OUTSIDE,* STRANGER.

THIS COULD BE THE BEGINNING OF A BEAUTIFUL FRIENDSHIP.

...NO NAME. NO MONEY. NO *I.D.*

WHAT IS THIS, FANCY DRESS?

I KNOW, IT'S KINDA WEIRD.

DOCTOR FLOSS SAID THE TAILORING LOOKED OLD, LIKE *COWBOY* CLOTHES.

BUT IT'S ALL *NEW*...

SO WHAT'S THE DEAL WITH THE ACTRESS LADY?

SHE PICKS UP INJURED MEN WHO LIKE TO DRESS IN *COSTUME?*

WHY WOULD SHE PAY FOR MY *TREATMENT* LIKE THAT?

ONE OF THE DOCTORS *CALLED* HER WHEN THEY BROUGHT YOU IN...

HOW ABOUT *THIS?*

WE DON'T HAVE TOO MUCH BACK HERE FOR GUYS YOUR *SIZE.*

I'LL LOOK LIKE A *GANGSTER!*

YOUR CHOICE, MUSCLES.

YOU CAN LOOK LIKE A *GANGSTER* OR YOU CAN LOOK LIKE A BARE-ASSED FUGITIVE...

*RETRO'S* BIG THIS YEAR, DIDN'T YOU HEAR?

AND LOOKING LIKE A CHUMP *NEVER* WENT OUT OF STYLE.

GIMME THAT.

So all I had to go on was cowboy clothes and an antique book.

Which, as it turned out, was plenty.

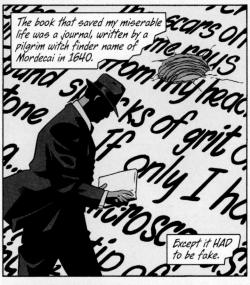

The book that saved my miserable life was a journal, written by a pilgrim witch finder name of Mordecai in 1640.

Except it HAD to be fake.

The paper was crumbling, for sure, but Mordecai's handwriting was modern, just like the way he put words together.

I could almost feel my entire body heat drain out through the soles of my feet when I figured out WHY there was something familiar about what I was reading.

The handwriting was MINE.

HEY, FELLAS.

I DON'T THINK THE LADY'S SIGNING AUTOGRAPHS RIGHT NOW.

UH, YEAH?

WHAT CAPACITY'S THAT?

EXPLAIN TO ME *AGAIN* HOW I GOT WRAPPED UP IN ALL THIS.

THIS IS A GAME OF *BLUFF*, AND I NEED YOU TO PLAY ALONG.

THERE'S AN *EXTRAVAGANT BOUQUET* IN THE *TRUNK*-- ALL *YOU* HAVE TO DO IS DISCREETLY DISPOSE OF THE ACCOMPANYING *CARD*.

IT'S FROM AN *ADMIRER*.

"JOHNNY."

WHO'S JOHNNY?

HE WANTS TO *DIRECT* ME IN A NEW MOVIE HE'S DOING CALLED *"THE BLACK GLOVE."*

*LIGHT*, DAMN YOU! *LIGHT!*

JOHN MAYHEW IS ONE OF THE RICHEST MEN IN AMERICA, AS YOU'D *KNOW* IF YOU WEREN'T SO STUBBORNLY *BLANK.*

"THE BLACK GLOVE"?

HE'S *MARRIED*, OF COURSE...BUT WHEN HAS *THAT* EVER STOPPED ME?

*OR* HIM.

LOOK, JUST SHOW ME YOU CAN *ACT* A LITTLE AND WE'LL BE FINE.

⋝SNF⋜

AND *YOU* ARE?

INTERNATIONAL GUILD OF PROFESSIONAL BUTLERS, AS A MATTER OF FACT.

BUTLER INSPECTOR.

IT'S A DIRTY JOB, I KNOW.

...I..I'M AFRAID... I...

THIS IS *NOT* THE TRADESMAN'S ENTRANCE, SIR.

I...I MUST ASK YOU TO LEAVE AT ONCE...I...

YOUR BIG PROBLEM RIGHT NOW IS MAKING IT THROUGH THIS *INSPECTION*.

TELL THE LADY OF THE HOUSE WE'RE *HERE* AND HOPE SHE MISSES THE COOK'S *LIPSTICK* ON YOUR SHIRT.

YOUR FLY'S OPEN, TOO.

...I... UMM...

FOR GOD'S SAKE, GROVES, PULL YOURSELF TOGETHER.

HE'S WITH *ME*.

GROVES?

GROVES, WHO'S THERE?

*BETSY!*

IT'S BEEN *EVER SO LONG* AND THEN I SAW THESE BEAUTIFUL FLOWERS AND *INSTANTLY* I THOUGHT OF *YOU!*

*MAY* WE?

...WELL, I *NEVER* TRUSTED HIM...BUT THEN THERE WAS THAT *TERRIBLE NIGHT*...

...AND EVERY TIME I THINK OF HIS *SNEERING*, *AWFUL* FACE...

⇗TSCHHA⇙ THE *WASPS* ARE THE *WORST* AT THIS TIME OF YEAR.

BUT NOW DEAR MARSHA'S TELLING ME YOU'RE A *DETECTIVE* AND THAT'S *EXACTLY* WHAT I NEED, MISTER... *UMM*...

YOU WERE *SAYING*... ABOUT THOMAS.

THOMAS *WAYNE*?

*AaUGHHH*

DON'T MIND *RODDY*, THAT'S HIS WAY OF SAYING *HELLO* AFTER THE *STROKE*...

FIRST HE SELLS *KANE CHEMICAL* TO *ACE* AND WE'RE *ALL SET* TO SPEND SOME *TIME* TOGETHER *THEN* IT'S *MARTHA* THEN IT'S *THIS*...

IF I CAN HELP FIND YOUR DAUGHTER'S *KILLER*, I WILL, MRS. KANE.

YOU SAY THOMAS WAYNE *PAID* TO HAVE YOUR DAUGHTER *MURDERED*, BUT...

OH, SO I'M SUPPOSED TO BELIEVE SHE *DIED* FOR THOSE *STUPID* PEARLS, IS THAT STILL THE STORY?

SOME *WORTHLESS* VAN DERM *HEIRLOOM*.

A *THIEF* WOULD *KNOW*.

A HIRED *ASSASSIN* WOULDN'T *CARE*.

WHEN TOMMY GAVE HER THOSE PEARLS AS AN *ANNIVERSARY* GIFT HE KNEW *EXACTLY* WHAT HE WAS DOING.

THE PEARLS WERE TO *IDENTIFY* HER TO THE GUNMAN.

*AUGHHHMMY*

RODDY, *PLEASE!*

YOUR HACKING AND CHOKING AND ROARING IS ADDING *NOTHING* TO THE CONVERSATION.

CHAUCHH

...AUUUMMY...

...DOO AUUUMMUS...

...GNNAUUURTT... PLFFS...

DOCTOR *THOMAS* BY DAY, *BAD TOMMY* AT NIGHT.

*PATRICK* AND *SILAS* HAD TO COVER UP THE *WHOLE THING.*

THE STOLEN *DRUGS,* THE *RAPE* CHARGES, THE *SECRET ROOM* WHERE THEY TREATED HIM FOR *MONTHS* WHILE MY GRANDSON WAS SENT AWAY TO A *BOARDING SCHOOL.*

HE *KILLED* MY DAUGHTER, OF THAT I HAVE NO DOUBT.

THEN HE *STOOD* THERE AND *ADMITTED* HE'D TURNED HER INTO A *DRUG ADDICT* AND... AND *WORSE*...

MAAUTHH

THOMAS WAYNE *TOLD* YOU THIS?

*AFTER* HIS ALLEGED DEATH?

SO WHO WAS WITH YOUR DAUGHTER OUTSIDE THE THEATER ON *PARK ROW* WHEN SHE WAS MURDERED?

WHOEVER *THAT* MAN WAS, IT WASN'T *TOM WAYNE!*

THOMAS WAYNE IS *ALIVE!*

LAUGHING AT ALL OF US!

HHUAURR AUURRT

HE'LL HAVE A NEW FACE NOW, A NEW NAME.

PLEASE FIND HIM.

HE KILLED MY LITTLE GIRL AND I DON'T KNOW WHAT TO DO.

WE'RE HOT ON THE *TRAIL,* BETSY.

BUT WE NEED THE KEYS TO *WAYNE MANOR...*

...I KNOW *YOU* HAVE A SET OF KEYS.

YOU...YOU'VE BEEN SUCH A *GOOD FRIEND* TO US...TO *MARTHA...*

DON'T EVER LET GOTHAM SPOIL YOUR SWEET NATURE.

THIS CITY'S HEART IS BLACK AND BROKEN.

WUMMAAUUTHA!

PLEASE, YOU *MUST* GO NOW. GROVES WILL SEE TO THE KEYS.

POOR RODDY. THAT'S THE *THING,* YOU SEE.

HE DOESN'T SEEM TO REALIZE OUR DARLING DAUGHTER IS *DEAD.*

THESE AWFUL WASPS.

THEY DON'T CARE, DO THEY?

WAYNE MANOR.

THEY HAD A *SON*, RIGHT?

HE WITNESSED THE *WHOLE* THING.

I DON'T SUPPOSE HE'LL *EVER* BE RIGHT.

THEY TOOK HIM AWAY ON A TRIP TO *HAWAII* OR *SOMETHING*.

PLACE HAS BEEN EMPTY FOR *MONTHS*.

THE KID.

THE KID DIDN'T STAY WITH HIS *GRAN'MA*.

WAS THERE A PROBLEM?

MARTHA'S RELATIONSHIP WITH HER FAMILY DETERIORATED *YEARS* AGO.

YOU *HEARD* HOW BETSY FELT ABOUT TOM WAYNE.

*YOU* KNEW THEM.

YOU REALLY *BELIEVE* THEY WERE *DEVIL WORSHIPPERS*?

HE *KILLED* HER AND FAKED HIS OWN DEATH?

IF HE *DID* HE'LL BE HERE TONIGHT.

HE'LL *DROP DEAD* WHEN HE SEES YOU.

*ENTREZ!*

THE *FAMILY PLOT?*

WHY HERE?

I THOUGHT WE'D START WITH A *HISTORY LESSON.*

THE WHOLE PILE SITS ON TOP OF AN *IMMENSE MAZE* OF *CAVES* THAT'S BEEN ASSOCIATED WITH *BURIED TREASURE* AND *ALL KINDS* OF ROMANTIC AND DEADLY CHARACTERS.

*JEREMY COE,* THE FRONTIERSMAN, *THE BLACK PIRATE,* THE *HELLERITE* SECT AND EVEN ANCIENT *BAT-PEOPLE.*

QUITE FRANKLY IF IT *WASN'T* BEING USED FOR SATANIC RITUALS, IT WOULD ALMOST SEEM A WASTE.

BAT-PEOPLE, HUH?

SO WHO'S *BURIED* HERE?

ALAN AND CATHERINE WAYNE.

"*DEEP INTO THAT DARKNESS, PEERING...*"

POE.

THIS DOOR'S BEEN *OPENED* RECENTLY.

YOU SAID THE PLACE HAD BEEN *EMPTY* FOR MONTHS.

AND IT *HAS,* BUT THIS EVENING IS THE TOTAL *ECLIPSE.*

AND I HAVE IT ON GOOD AUTHORITY THAT SOMETHING WILL *HAPPEN* HERE TONIGHT.

BUT FIRST...

...WE HAVE *ONE LAST STOP* TO MAKE.

WILLOWOOD MILITARY PSYCHIATRIC HOSPITAL.

...MY METHODS ARE ABOUT *HELPING* SERVICEMEN AND WOMEN TO *RELIVE* THOSE TRAUMATIC MOMENTS AND...AND...FIND *HEALING*...

...I CAME TO WILLOWOOD TO HELP PEOPLE.

THE *TIME HYPNOSIS* TECHNIQUE IS THE *LEAST* OF WHAT YOU HAVE TO OFFER YOUR COUNTRY, CARTER.

WHAT ABOUT YOUR PATENT APPLICATIONS FOR *PROBABILITY VIEWERS*, PORTABLE *TIME TRAVEL FIELD GENERATORS*?

YOU COULD BE THE *RICHEST MAN ON EARTH.*

YOU *KNOW* WHO I AM.

I'M OFFERING *YOU* THE SAME DEAL I OFFERED THE *OTHERS*.

AND I BET YOU *EVERYTHING* YOU CAN'T REFUSE.

TELL ME THAT'S NOT *HESITATION*, CARTER.

IF YOU DON'T WANT THE *WEALTH*, THE *FAME*, THE ADMIRATION OF YOUR PEERS...

...WHAT ABOUT THE *WOMAN*?

...ULMM...

THE...*UH*...THE *TIMEBOX* ALONE WOULD REQUIRE *FIVE GIGAWATTS* OF POWER TO DUH-DO WHAT YOU'RE ASKING, *DOCTOR*...

...THAT KIND OF POWER IS... BEYOND... BEYOND...

THINK ABOUT WHAT HAPPENED WHEN *RODERICK KANE* CHOSE NOT TO PLAY.

BUT DON'T THINK *TOO* LONG.

YOUR *VISITOR* WON'T KEEP FOREVER.

BATMAN BEWARE

THE HOLE IN THINGS

EXCUSE ME?

HE...ER...YOU MUST HAVE MISHEARD...

...HE *CAN'T* ACTUALLY SPEAK...

...THE WAR.

CARTER, YOU *MUST* MEET MY NEW FRIEND.

HE'S HELPING ME UNRAVEL ALL *KINDS* OF MYSTERIES.

NICE TO MEET YOU, PROF.

HAVE WE MET SOMEWHERE *BEFORE?*

...I...I... DON'T... URMM...

*CARTER NICHOLS* IS THE MODERN *EINSTEIN*, BUT SOMETIMES I HAVE TO WRESTLE HIM AWAY FROM HIS TOP SECRET *TIME TRAVEL* RESEARCH.

HE AND THOMAS WERE FRIENDS AT *SCHOOL*...

WHAT *IS* THAT YOU'RE READING?

A STORY CLOSE TO MY *HEART*, YOU COULD SAY.

THE PLOT'S GOT A FEW *HOLES*, BUT I THINK IT'S STARTING TO MAKE SENSE.

WHAT DID I *TELL* YOU?

COMMISSIONER LOEB, MAYOR JESSOP...

THESE ARE SOME OF GOTHAM'S MOST *POWERFUL* MEN.

AND THEY'RE *ALL* PART OF THIS.

THIS *WHAT?*

WHY A *BAT,* MARSHA?

WHY *ME?*

I WAS *RUNNING OUT OF TIME* AND *YOU* WERE THE BEST OF THREE POTENTIAL TALL, DARK AND HANDSOMES.

THE COSTUME'S BASED ON SOMETHING THOMAS WAYNE WORE TO A *PARTY...*

SO WE STARE ACCUSINGLY, DRESSED AS THE GHOSTS OF THE WAYNES AND *THEN* WHAT?

SOME RICH SATANIST DROPS TO HIS KNEES AND *CONFESSES* TO MURDER?

LIKE THE ONE WHO SENT THOSE HOODS TO THE HOSPITAL?

HOW DID THEY KNOW YOU WERE THERE, ANYWAY?

IF THEY KILLED THE *WAYNES,* WHAT MAKES YOU OR ME ANY DIFFERENT?

TOO MANY QUESTIONS.

I ONLY ASKED YOU TO *PLAY* A DETECTIVE.

SO MAYBE SOMETHING DOESN'T ADD UP.

YOU'RE NOT TELLING ME THE *WHOLE* STORY, MARSHA.

THESE PEOPLE *KILLED MY DEAREST FRIEND.*

IF I HAVE TO GO DOWN THERE *ALONE,* I WILL.

BUT *YOU'RE* NOT THE SORT TO TURN YOUR BACK ON A DAMSEL IN DISTRESS, ARE YOU?

MY DARK KNIGHT.

THERE'S MORE.

LATER.

DARK KNIGHT.

WHEN I MARRY *JOHNNY MAYHEW,* YOU CAN BE MY *CHAUFFEUR...*

REMEMBER, THE CLOCK STRIKES *SEVEN* AND *TOTALITY* BEGINS.

*I was getting closer to something big.*

*It felt like a cold tide of black water spiraling around a drain.*

Playing a ghost didn't seem so bad.

My head already felt like the hallway of a haunted house.

And I couldn't help thinking I'd done this before.

NO ONE WILL GET *HURT,* WILL THEY?

NO ONE *IMPORTANT,* CARTER.

NO ONE WHO *MATTERS.*

AND PLEASE...

...MY NAME HERE IS *BROTHER SIMON.*

*BARBATOS* WILL LEAD US TO THE HIDDEN *CASKET OF IMMORTALITY* AND *LIFE ETERNAL.*

ALL IS PREPARED...

...FOR THE *CEREMONY OF THE BAT.*

FETCH YOUR *CAMERA,* BROTHER JOHN.

Director. Lights, camera, action.

There was only one thing missing.

MARSHA.

MARSHA?

UNNH!

A DRIFTER.

A MAN NO ONE WILL MISS.

COME FORWARD, ANOINTED ONE.

It was somewhere around about then I had the whole thing worked out.

But that didn't make it hurt any less.

Anointed.

That explained the tingling in my lips all the way back to my brain.

A poison kiss.

200 YEARS AGO *BARBATOS* WAS BEYOND OUR ABILITIES TO *EXPLAIN* OR COMPREHEND-- A DEMON, A MYTH.

NOW WE HAVE DARK SCIENCE ON OUR SIDE.

A NEW UNDERSTANDING OF *TIME* AND UNEARTHLY LIFEFORMS.

*I heard voices but the drug let only fragments through, like surrealist telegrams.*

A SACRIFICIAL VICTIM.

GOTHAM GOAT-HOME.

A SCAPEGOAT DEVIL.

THE *HUMAN BAT.*

FOOTAGE OF *MARTHA WAYNE* COMMITTING *MURDER!*

OF A *DETECTIVE* HIRED BY HER PARENTS!

A MAN'S SOUL IS IN HIS *REPUTATION*, HIS *LEGACY.*

DESTROY A REPUTATION, DESTROY A *SOUL.*

DOCUMENTARY EVIDENCE AGAINST THE *WAYNES* AND THEIR *BUTLER.* FAKE PHOTOGRAPHS. LETTERS.

SOULS TO FEED *BARBATOS.*

NO ONE LOST A SOUL BUT *YOU*, MARSHA.

YOU DON'T NEED TO DO THIS.

HMFF.

I was weak as a radio signal coming in from the Andromeda galaxy.

A splash of gasoline cologne added the Man About Town touch and I was ready for my close-up.

TOTALITY APPROACHES!

IN THE NAME OF THE *FIRST RED ROCK* AND THE *RAGE,* AND THE ANGELS AND DUKES OF THE DARK SIDE *INFERNO PITS.*

...MARSHA...

...DON'T *DO* THIS...

...TELL THEM TO STOP.

SAVE YOUR BREATH.

I'D DO *ANYTHING* TO NEVER GROW OLD.

AND IT'S *MARTHA.*

LOOK, RODDY, LOOK!

ALL THE BELLS ARE RINGING, TOO.

≥KCCHHH≤

OPEN THE HOLE IN TIME, CARTER, AND MAKE HISTORY.

THE POWER YOU NEED IS YOURS.

CALL DOWN BARBATOS, THE HUNTER, THE FINDER OF GREAT TREASURE!

...NO...

I WON'T DO THIS.

I DON'T WANT ANY PART OF YOUR BLACK GLOVE.

The way out was always right in front of me.

DON'T

DON'T LOOK AT ME THAT WAY.

It started with a dame.

It ended with a funeral.

And the only way out was in a BOX.

I must have known that one all along.

What I could never have expected was what happened NEXT...and what I became, there at the end.

RODDY?

...NO...

MY DISCOVERIES ARE NOT FOR SALE.

MY SOUL IS NOT FOR SALE.

DOES THIS MEAN I WIN YOUR WAGER, DOCTOR HURT?

YES, I THINK IT DOES, CARTER. WELL DONE.

I HOPE THAT THOUGHT WILL COMFORT YOU IN THE YEARS OF LONELY OBSCURITY AHEAD.

NOW RUN.

WHERE DID HE GO?

WHAT HAPPENED?

YOU SAID ETERNAL LIFE...

the local timeline terminates in **12 minutes.**

THIS *ARCHIVE*... IT'S THE ENTIRE *HISTORY* OF THE *UNIVERSE* DOWN TO EVERY MICROSCOPIC DETAIL, THE MOST PRECIOUS THING *EVER.*

AND YOU'RE *BUSH ROBOTS*...

...ADAPTED FOR A *STERILE* ENVIRONMENT, WOULD I BE RIGHT?

while **you** are the solution to one of history's great **mysteries.**

the first human **deep time probe** vanished on its maiden voyage.

over several thousand millennia we searched for the nichols engine in every era--a hole-- a gap in the archive.

UNTIL *IT* BROUGHT *ME* HERE.

OKAY, SO HERE'S THE QUESTION... ...WHERE DO I FIND A *TIME MACHINE* TO GET ME OUT OF HERE AND *BACK HOME?*

it would **consume** our resources and hasten the **destruction** of vanishing point--but an **escape module** could be constructed by **evolving** the nichols engine.

construction time: **10 minutes.**

the **penultimate** significant event--the arrival of superman's **search party**--will have occurred by then.

BY WHICH TIME DARKSEID'S *HYPER-ADAPTER* WILL BE *FREE.* I CAN'T LET IT WREAK HAVOC WITH THE ARCHIVE.

I NEED A *DISGUISE.*

AND ONCE YOU HEAR WHAT I HAVE TO *SAY,* YOU'LL KNOW WHY I NEED YOU TO TAKE AWAY MY *MEMORY* AGAIN.

I accept my **sacrifice,** pre-ordained by the archive.

may I say how honored I am to be a significant part of batman's final adventure... and his **new** beginning.

commence **time sphere** assembly.

NEW BEGINNING?

assume **bi-organic** configuration.

the local timeline terminates in **11 minutes 17 seconds.**

an infestation of **hyperfauna** has been detected.

*The sound of ancient, rusty locks unlatching.*

...WE'RE *LOCKED* ONTO MY *OWN* STOLEN TIME SPHERE.

MY GOD, I THINK THE ARCHIVISTS WERE *REBOOTING* THE UNIVERSE...USING THE *BLACK HOLE* TO *LOOP* THE TIMELINE'S *END* THROUGH ITS *BEGINNING*...

...THE ENGINE WILL *FIRE* WITH MINIMAL *HEAT ENERGY*...

STRAP YOURSELVES IN FOR THE MOTHER OF *ALL RIDES.*

IT'S THE HEAT DEATH OF THE UNIVERSE.

EVEN *BODY TEMPERATURE'S* A SUPER-FEAT.

BUT HERE GOES.

WE'RE HEADING THROUGH THE *EYE OF THE NEEDLE OF TIME!*

HOLD YOUR BREATH, GUYS, HERE IT *COMES*...

THE BIG ALL-OVER!

MAYBE I'LL FINALLY REMEMBER WHO I *AM*.

THE POWER OF THE MAGIC LASSO CAN BE NEITHER *BROKEN* NOR *RESISTED*.

TELL ME HOW YOU CAME TO *BE* HERE, LIKE *THIS*...

I WORKED IT ALL OUT TO *SAVE* EVERYONE.

BUT I HAD TO *FORGET* SO THAT THE *HYPER-ADAPTER* WOULD HAVE NOTHING TO GO ON.

I *TRICKED* IT INTO COMING HERE TO *THIS* DAY, THIS MOMENT.

*MOTHER* ...AYED YOU! MOTHER ...IED! MOTHER BOX LIED! ...LL HER *NOTHING*! ...OTHER *NOTHING*!

NOTHING.

I'M BRUCE WAYNE.

NOW IT *KNOWS*.

I NEED YOUR *HELP*, DIANA.

*FATHER* ...TED YOU! STAY ...ONELY! STAY DEAD ...OREVER FATHER FEAR!

HE'S TELLING THE *TRUTH*.

BUT... THERE'S *MORE*.

THERE'S SOMETHING *ELSE*, ISN'T THERE?

WHAT *IS* IT? WHAT'S THAT WEIRD DOUBLE ECHO?

I'M GETTING *HARDCORE* DEJÁ VU...

*PROTECT* YOURSELF, TIM.

GODS AND *NEW GODS* LIKE *DARKSEID* ARE SELF-AWARE *IDEAS*. THEY USE *CONCEPT-WEAPONS*, ANTI-LIFE *EQUATIONS*, HUNTER-KILLER *METAPHORS*.

I KNOW *YOU'RE* TELLING THE TRUTH, BRUCE...

...NOW LET THE *ARCHIVIST* SPEAK.

... "HYPER-ADAPTER"...

...HUNTER-KILLER...A LIVING *CURSE* MADE TO DESTROY *BATMAN* AND THE *WORLD*...

...A *"DEATH-IDEA"* THAT NEVER TIRES, NEVER *STOPS*...

...BUT THE SPHERE'S RIGGED TO BLOW AND TURN IT *BACK* ON ITSELF.

IT'S SEALED *INSIDE!*

...take control... adapt...

...escape... return... destroy...

TIME SPHERE *SELF-DESTRUCT.*

ENGAGE.

Whatever they touch turns to myth.

Understand that much.

HE'S BEEN *CLINICALLY DEAD* FOR *TWO MINUTES.*

OMEGA RADIATION IS *LEAVING* HIS BODY AND WE HAVE ONLY MOMENTS TO *REVIVE* HIM WHEN IT'S GONE.

PRAY TO *APHRODITE* HE STILL HAS THE *STRENGTH* TO COME BACK FROM THE *LAND OF SHADES* IN *HADES.*

I KNOW HOW TO BRING HIM BACK.

TELL HIM GOTHAM'S IN *TROUBLE.*

AND TELL HIM HE'LL NEED *THIS.*

It's not over.

GOTCHA!

250 years ago, the hyper-adapter infected a human host. A pure strain of platonic evil.

START HIS HEART!

There's still time to stop it.

The first truth of Batman...

It had to be one I don't like to admit.

The gunshots left me alone.

For years I was alone in the echoing dark of that well.

But something else defined the exact moment Batman was born.

The first truth of Batman...

The saving grace.

I was never alone.

GGAUGGH

I had help.

# BACK IN TIME

## THE RETURN OF BRUCE WAYNE SKETCHBOOK

Grant Morrison • Andy Kubert • Chris Sprouse
Frazer Irving • Yanick Paquette • Ryan Sook

This page: A sampling of thumbnail layouts by Grant Morrison for issue #6.

Opposite: Morrison's character design for the Archivist.

to FRAZER IRVING

# ARCHIVIST — RETURN OF BRUCE WAYNE ②

SOLID BLACK
ith 'Shaggy'
effect of
endrils

'BUSH ROBOT'
FRACTAL 'ARMS'
+ MULTI-FINGERS

look like tree
branches made
of black
wire

they can
plug into any
equipment
and for
gripping

glides
on
fractal feat

Pencilled outtakes and character designs by Chris Sprouse.

Top: A variant cover art sketch by Chris Sprouse for issue #1.

Above: Andy Kubert's thumbnail roughs for the series' covers.

Opposite: Character designs by Andy Kubert for the cover art to issues #1-2

• DEAD BAT USED TO
HOLD CAPE ON
OVER
SHOULDERS

• UTILITY BELT CONSISTS
OF POUCHES, CLAWS,
TWINE/VINES +
HAMMER/AXE
ATTACHED

• GAUNLETS HAVE CLAWS
EMBEDDED AND ARE
MADE OUT OF
LEATHER

• LEGGINGS MADE OUT
OF LEATHER & STITCHED
HELD ON WITH TWINE

...KLES (SHOES, HAT)
... BAT SYMBOLS

...H BELT IS
...ILITY BELT/
...CHES, CAPSULES,
...OPE.

• HIGH
COLLAR
ON CAPE/COV...

Left and opposite: Examples of art progression on two panels from issue #2 by Frazer Irving.

Above: Irving's preliminary color sketch for issue #2's variant cover art.

Opposite and left: Pirate studies by Yanick Paquette for issue #3.

Below: Andy Kubert's character designs for the cover art to issue #3.

POINTED HAT

BANDANA/MASK

HIGH COLLAR

'DREADLOCK' BEARD

BELT W/ POUCHES

POINTED BLACK GLOVES

'SCALLOPED' BOTTOM OF COAT... BUTTONS/ UNDER-COAT IS BLACK W/ BLACK SCALLOPS

BLACK SASH/ FRAYED ENDS

BLACK BOOTS

Andy Kubert

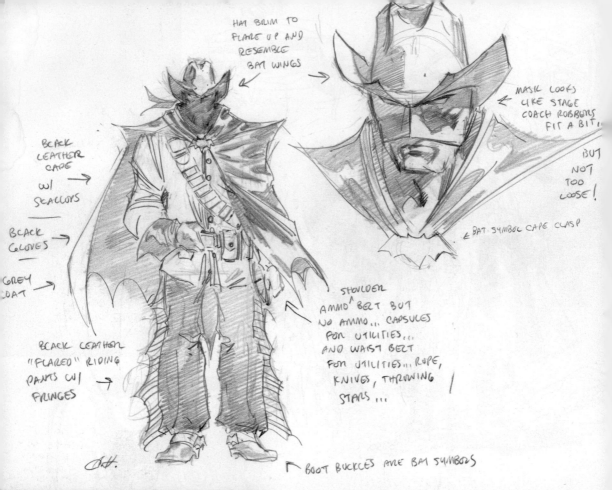

HAT BRIM TO
FLARE UP AND
RESEMBLE
BAT WINGS

MASK LOOKS
LIKE STAGE
COACH ROBBERS
FIT A BIT

BUT
NOT
TOO
LOOSE!

BLACK
LEATHER
CAPE
W/
SCALLOPS

BLACK
GLOVES

GREY
COAT

BLACK LEATHER
"FLARED" RIDING
PANTS W/
FRINGES

← BAT SYMBOL CAPE CLASP

SHOULDER
AMMO BELT BUT
NO AMMO... CAPSULES
FOR UTILITIES...
AND WAIST BELT
FOR UTILITIES... ROPE,
KNIVES, THROWING
STARS...

BOOT BUCKLES ARE BAT SYMBOLS

Above and right: Character designs by Andy Kubert for issue #4's cover art.

Opposite top: An unused Victorian Batman design by Kubert.

Opposite bottom: Kubert's gangster Batman designs for the cover art to issue #5.

BLACK
DUSTER
JACKET W/
SCALLOPS

BLACK
GLOVES

BLACK BOOTS W/
BAT SYMBOLS

R.O.B.W. VICTORIANBRUCE//

TOP HAT BRIM SHAPED TO RESEMBLE BAT EARS

VICTORIAN TIE W/BATSYMBOL

EMBLEM ON JACKET TO RESEMBLE BAT

WIDE UTILITY BELT W/ POUCHES/ CHAIN W/ POUCHES

CAPE SCALLOPED

BLACK HAT POINTED BRIM IN FRONT + SLIGHTLY UPTURNED ON SIDES (EARS)

BLACK COAT/ UPTURNED SHOULDERS

BOTTON

VEST W/ BAT SYMBOL

ARM-CUFFS W/ GAUNTLET TYPE DESIGN

"UTILITY" BELT WORN LIKE SHOULDER HOLSTERS W/ BATARANGS, CAPSULES, POUCHES, ROPE

SCALLOPED BOTTOM EDGE OF COAT

BLACK PANTS + SHOES

BRUCE HAS SLICKED UP/ COMBED BACK

Andy Kubert

Left: A color sketch by Ryan Sook for issue #5's variant cover art.

Below and following pages: Selected page layout thumbnails by Ryan Sook for issue #5.

TURN
ON LAM

CAPTION
BECOMES →
B.GROUND